MORE THAN OKAY

Poetry of Wellness

LORRAINE J. DORIVAL

WESTBOW
PRESS®
A DIVISION OF THOMAS NELSON
& ZONDERVAN

WestBow Press books may be ordered through booksellers or by contacting:

WestBow Press
A Division of Thomas Nelson & Zondervan
1663 Liberty Drive
Bloomington, IN 47403
www.westbowpress.com
844-714-3454

Musical Manuscript transcribed by Robert Owen.

ISBN: 979-8-3850-0161-3 (sc)
ISBN: 979-8-3850-0163-7 (hc)
ISBN: 979-8-3850-0162-0 (e)

Library of Congress Control Number: 2023912706

Print information available on the last page.

WestBow Press rev. date: 8/24/2023

Also Book by Author

YOU IN ME.

Contents

Dedication

This poetry collection is dedicated to those of us in the process of making life changes and those of us still considering whether to make those changes. May we take courage and be strengthened in our endeavours.

Preface

I do not mean to be disrespectful, but I think I contracted COVID19 in the year 2023 after receiving two vaccinations and a booster shot.

A hacking cough had kept me up all night and the following morning found me listless and drowsy. Some friends had reported that they had contracted COVID with similar symptoms and suggested that I ought to take an antigen test to confirm whether I was negative or positive. The antigen test box and its many instructions seemed more ominous than the way I was feeling, so decided to bear my ailment without much fuss. After all, my malaise started with flu symptoms of a common cold and sore throat. So, if this was COVID, there was not much to the sickness, I thought. I would quarantine for five to ten days anyway in sympathy with the winter weather with its heavy snow falls and freezing rain.

COVID consumed three years of our lives and that time was referred to as before COVID and after COVID. That pandemic affected the world in many ways. Some people suffered mild attacks and thought nothing of them. Some with pre-existing conditions received fatal attacks which ended their suffering and left loved ones bereft. The pandemic created havoc with millions of people dying globally and tens of thousands left in various forms of incapacitation. That was not the extent of its effect. The pandemic brought sudden changes in the work place and in the home space. Some people took the opportunity to reflect on their lives and give themselves new directions.

Some blame COVID for everything- a mere common cold, their long accustomed periodic headaches. COVID got blamed for anything nowadays. Questions of career changes and choices were explored. The strains of long struggling relationships grew quite weak forcing decisions to love stronger or to go their separate ways. Some infused more laughter and play in their lives and some felt that the next best thing was to tie the knot in marriage.

Like most people, my days in locked-down gave me the opportunity to clean out my space. This also entailed reviewing files and old manuscripts and throwing out redundancies. I came upon a bunch of work which I had collected over decades and had quite forgotten. I know that I had done the work and marvelled that I had been in that curious head space to have conceived such inspired work. I wanted to explore further.

Thus, resumed poetry writing. The writing took me on a course highlighted by my experiences and a need to live more consciously. The first book entitled "You in Me" is a journey of healing and growth through spirituality and relationships. This second book "More Than Okay" is a continuation of poems on wellness seen through the lens of a homecoming arena. Both bodies of work address situations which could aid in experiencing our best lives now.

These situations can be best understood by examining the habits with which we occupy ourselves and how honorably we engage in the celebration of life.

The coaching discussions and exercises included at the end of the book are for the purpose of assisting you further in your wellness explorations.

I hope you will be inspired and find value in the work, as I have been inspired. Also, enjoy the reading as I have enjoyed the writing.

Acknowledgement

I offer sincere gratitude to my dear friends Anne Hurtubise, Louise Labelle, Marybeth Roblin and Ligia Teisan. Their strong emotional reaction to my reading of the poems encouraged me to keep on writing.

Homecoming

Tour Of Love & Life
(Our Native Land)

Lorraine Dorival

stretch out_____ for miles_____ re - veal - ing trea-sures of_____

_____ the deep_____ And we wind through bus - hy ways_____

_____ of mul - ti col-oured fo li - age_____ Rain - bows gleamed on mis - ty ha - ze_____

_____ And we climbed down val - ley mounds Where nat - ive youths and beauts a - bound

Midst nat - ure's va - ried joy - ous so - unds My tour of end - less warmth._____

_____ Awe - some moun - tain peaks_____ Hold ben - ign se-crets,

Heard on - ly by lu mi-nous flies_____ Blue oc - eans gorge Fed by e - merald

D.C. al Fine

falls Their riv - ers gurg - ling down to shore._____

Small Trials

In life, we have to learn how to be happy.
Happy is a state of mind,
Preceded by internal peace.
Both are daily practises until perfected.
Mind your influences and experiences.
Watch your thoughts and feelings.
No one can make you happy.
No one can induce your inner peace.
Neither of these can be found
Outside ourselves.

***

When something pains you,
You have been treated unkindly
And discourteously,
Take a stance and be aware,
Know that the pain is there.
Greet it, acknowledge it, and
Ask what have you done to so
Deserve, and listen for the answer.
Breathe, breathe through the pain
Inhale, Ahhhhhhhhhhhhhhhh.
Exhale, Phewwwwwwwwww.
And the pain is gone.
All is forgiven.

***

You want me to pin your portrait
All over my walls like giant works of art.
Is this vanity or what?

***

We all experience pain.
How then would we know happiness
Without acknowledging its opposite, pain?
Pain is a part of life.
As we justify our actions
And misunderstand others,
Give the pain its real name.
Own it and process it,
Lest we project it onto others
And have them bear ours
As well as endure their own.

***

Dysfunction is not the ability to have
And express an opinion.
It is the inflexibility with which the opinion
Is held and expressed.
As though, this opinion is the only truth
And all have to abide by it.
As though no other truth exists.

***

Thousands of words jump around
Fleeting through my agile brain,
Tumbling, intertwining and incoherent
Difficult to coordinate and put together,
Scrambling, they often lose their meaning.

So, don't laugh at my composing
And give them meaning unintended,
Nor snicker at constant misspelling.
Just gloss the words for your own learning.

***

My inner knowing reveals my true way.
I am awestruck by its trajectory.
When obeyed, I reap the divine rewards.
Otherwise, I live to struggle another day.

***

The poet's thoughts
Give fresh insight into the workings
Of the mind and heart.
And an opening to productive discourse
About what the world could become.

***

When things are going fine,
It means that the stars are aligned.
Take the opportunities benign
As precious gifts from the divine.
When things don't seem right,
You will not see stars bright.
Change direction, keep out-of-sight
And wait for the new light.

***

There is no one else like you.
You are special and unique.
And have been assigned a divine role.

As you focus on your assignment,
It will be divinely designed.

***

Walking in comfortable shoes,
Boosts the beauty of that walk.
Wearing old broken shoes,
Dispels ultimate confidence.
Moving with beauty and grace,
Expresses comfort and confidence.

***

Perfection only recognizes
The "im" in im-perfection
To guide, sustain and transform.
Im. I'm meaning " Myself" desiring perfection.
Im is the awareness with which we conduct ourselves.
Im guides us in ways of perfection.
Im sustains us during the process of perfection.
Im transforms the self to perfection.

***

Though you occupy less than one-trillionth
Of an inch of space in the universe,
The universe needs you for its completion.
Though you spend less than one-trillionth
Of a minute on planet earth,
Planet earth needs your time for its revolution.
Your time and space are important in the equation.
They are necessary for enlightenment and rejuvenation.
And need your love and life to fulfil the whole.

***

Writing My Poems

Now comes my turn to recite a poem
Of verses intensely bold and bright
And lyrics commingling the dance of life.

I searched the sonnets unabridged
For tales of love and spring and peace.
Alas! My memory n'er diction give.

Maybe, a choice at frolic, song or dance;
My muddy thoughts have gone askance.
Procrastination no longer stands.

So tested the rhythm as I wrote some lines,
And dreamed of poets liking my rhymes.
Perchance, your heartbeats mark my time!

I write my poems with tongue in cheek
In total awe of what comes from me
And wondered how much could there be?

Do not judge me and my poems,
They are inspired for our learning and growth
And help to express my creative girth.

The creative girth is extensive
And awaits the search for inspiration
And brings out what lies dormant within.

Searching the mind to be inspired,
Allowing all creativity to shine.
Then write the poetry for all time.

Now is the time to write your poems.
As the heart speaks of its needs
And the head forgives misdeeds.

Writing your poetry will release
Much of what your heart conceives
As you align with inner spirit deeds.

Surprise yourself and everybody else,
As the spirit manifests through you
And you write poetry as it leads.

See beauty in the words.
Glean wisdom from the thoughts.
And feel joy in the delivery.

The rhythm of words will enchant you.
The truth in thoughts will inform you
And the glory of delivery will transport you

***

Undeserved Punishment

Crying, shouting and wailing
Heard through the railings
As his manic yelling
punctuated paddle beating
"Adultery. Is. Not. Acceptable!"
She was taken completely
By surprise.
What on earth was
He talking about?
What had got into him?
He had never done this before.
His wife had stopped
To talk to a man.
Not interested in whom it was,
He just wanted to beat
The daylights out of her.
"You are right", she yelled back.
"Nothing going on!"
"Cousin Joe and I were saying.
How well the business was doing."
Joe was his chief investor
And favourite relative.
Joe continuously followed
The progress of the business.
He suddenly stopped
His ranting and raving
And listened.
"Think of what you are doing,"
She said, "This is abuse!
"And that's wrong,

"Both physically and emotionally."
He became repentant
And promised never to do that again.
"Let this be the only time.
Or I'll call the police."

Crossing Over

Using the road less travelled to go across,
She wavered laboriously and haltingly.
Wading waist high in a river of slime
To reach sheltered space in record time.
She has crossed, waiting for my climb.

Choosing her short way seemed dangerous.
I took the other looking less treacherous.
Cautiously walking unfamiliar pathways,
Met surprising obstacles along the by-ways,
Hidden amidst lengthy walking trailways.

Arriving at a gushing stream of melted snow,
Wondered, 'was it safe to cross, stand or go?'
Realized that route will take twice as long.
As I treaded slimy ground of muck and mud,
And risked a plunge in that cold water tub.

Trying to avoid mounds of old snow,
I climbed huge brown mossy shores.
Treaded on thin ice, kicked snow balls,
Wiped off shoes on moist grassy knolls.
Encountered stumbling blocks big and small.

Coming upon obstacles here and there,
Caused confusion to proceed somewhere.
The objective was to cross nice and easy
To reach the other side in time not busy
Not to wade in dangerous waters so tizzy!

Crossing over can involve some risks.
A decision to make valuable disks,
Expecting the land to lay low and fallow,
Not hidden dangers with turns so shallow.
Challenges occur to help us learn and grow.

Expecting to reach a safe and secure place,
Had not anticipated such a challenging race.
Obstacles surprisingly appeared everywhere.
But successful crossing requires positive care.
To guide the crossing with trust to prosper.

Crossing will conquer regardless of pace.
And requires patience, courage and grace,
Happening in reasonable time and space.
The time secured by God's saving grace
And space provided for every positive face.

***

The Park

Love the park!
Live a stone's throw from High Park.
Commune with nature in the park.
Watch others communion in the park.

Everything happens in High Park.
It is so open and inviting.
You can see much in daylight,
As you see in the dark.

Children fleet around on slippery sliding skids,
Chasing each other like waterpark kids.
Yelling, wetting others in frightened glee.
A mother scolds her child for misdeeds.
Father playfully pushes son on the swing.
Toddlers get ready for water ramp slide.
A group awaits a turn on the merry-go-round.
As some splash gayly in the wading pond.

A spanking new deck with rails was built,
Where fishing became the sport of quilts.
Frustrated by intrusion of fishing lines,
Ducks retaliated with protesting quacks
And generously littered the grounds around.
I gingerly trod through droppings of ducks,
Considered which of several trails for luck
And approached a display of coloured docks.

Cuddling mothers sat in cherry tree shades,
Swinging in hammocks and watching charades.
Groups of persons adorned the mounds.
Children chasing the ducks round and round.
Scouts meeting here and band practice there.

Engaged readers and interesting strollers;
Curious toddlers escaping their guards,
While picking flowers and feeding the birds,
Forbidden activities a despairing scold.

The touring trams ride the main tracks,
Of the dozens of trails in High Park.
The tram drivers quite enjoy their task,
As they wave cheerfully making their trek.
A ride in a tram gives great over views;
Boys playing basket ball and soccer dues;
Huge swimming pools with rookie swimmers;
Anxious parents cheering on their winners.

A ride through the forests and shady hills,
Gives a glimpse of the zoo and its many thrills.
You surprisingly arrive at the public streets.
You're invited to attend the theatrical plays
But choose instead to watch tennis displays.
And stop by the fields of girls' softball play.
Young men are having the time of their lives
Coaching their young and shielding their hides.

Your horticultural studies have just begun,
Naming the plants and admiring blossoms.
Attending a class or a nursery lesson.
Educational events always in session.
The occasional odd buildings house
Offices, schools and recreational sites.
While spectators stood by fenced rites
Observing the coaching and tennis likes.

Done my trek up and down hills and vales,
Stopping, staring, enjoying, admiring.
As dusk approached, police set up blocks
To keep out the night of after dark sports.
Already had a glimpse of such happenings
Before they were guided out off the gates.
My communion in nature continues today.
I am energized, refreshed and renewed in spirit.

Enjoying High Park

Carnival

Carnival, a time of release
Making way for spiritual
Rejuvenation and renewal.
National celebration evolving,
Paradoxically remains the same.
Freedom seeking and ever revolving
Yesteryear becomes today again.

Rising gaiety festoons the air,
Causing joyousness everywhere.
Music, laughter, noise and play.
Festivals grace streets and stays.
Again, nature's scenes enjoining
Multiple interpretations creating.
Elders and toddlers join the fray.

Year-round busy preparations
Forge vivacious competitions,
Beauty, Calypso and music steelpans,
Decorated floats, costumes and bands.
Awards are granted of exotic trips
And fully paid University scholarships.
As determined competitors vie their best
To win world wide open contests.

Not too long now to await the days.
Sturdy *glorisida* branches whittled.
Grandma's vintage nighties settled.
Brother's favourite worn-out pants
Become teen majorettes' waving flags.
Sequinned costumes and crocus bags,
Coloured ribbons and frivolous bows
Ready for playing in orderly rows.

Patrons line town and country streets,
For long awaited parade feats.
Sidewalks and roads laced by food carts
Enticing all to come spend some cash.
Musical bands strike favourite tunes,
Expecting theirs to be road match.
Revellers all ready in jump-up catch.

Floats and bands in sparkling array
Depict nature in a variety of ways.
Painted bodies show energetic displays
Of imaginative places and funny plays.
Responding to nature's perpetual call,
Jubilance rise like the noon day sun
And happiness spills out all around.

Carnival once again draws love,
Love for all and all for love.
Love with music, song and dance.
Dance in all proportions and stance.
Wining, twirling, whirling, twisting,
Stilting, swaying, playing, gyrating,
To infectious stanza, all are jumping.

Music blasting, blowing, strumming,
Drumming pulsing through the being.
Music reverberating in joyous grace
Songs filling up every hallow space.
Start the rejuvenation of every face,
Transforming yesteryear's low disgrace.
All ecstatically dance at their own pace.

Joyous air enthralled in high spirits.
Some, aided by a few grogs of rum,
Exuberantly embracing one and all.
Expressing released carnival lore.
Music seeping through opened cores.
A marvelous display of spontaneity and art
To liven the spirit and sooth the heart.

Revelling dwindles at end of day,
When music, song and dance are sated.
Significant others seek out each other
And some new friendships commit forever.
You hear the chip, chip, chip of tired feet
Slowed to the rhythm of closing music.
Another carnival enjoyed and gone
Looking forward to the next one to come.

***

Averie Arthur (2 years old)
Toronto Carnival Princess 2023

Sister Mary Theophana

Everyone spoke so lovingly of her.
They shared appreciative good memories
Of her dynamic influences with all,
And special ways she touched our lives.

We kept up a lifetime of communication
To give news of her old CHS students.
Everyone thought herself the favourite
And always wanted some news of her.

Called Elsa or Theo by her friends,
A familiarity only allowed by some.
She radiated strong capacity to love
Showing interest in and goodwill to all.

She approached her life with exuberance,
Abiding by her daily remembrance
To express gladness wherever she went,
In fulfillment of her divine testament.

Her enthusiasm inspired us to perform
Our very best and beyond comfort zone.
She singled me unexpectedly at odd times
Being one of the more introverted in class.

She never showed debilitated energy.
Interested herself in my personal growth.
At all times urging me on courageously,
Electing me captain of The Crown Girls.

Her extravert challenged my introvert,
Persuading me to exercise judgement,
Choosing the leaders for the group.
Often trying my many inefficiencies.

She understood most introverts
Performed well in theatre and on stage.
Relentlessly coached us to excellence.
A great accomplishment for her students.

Despite her intentional persuasion,
I was often a source of great irritation,
Disobediently acting lines undefined.
But eventually followed her directions.

Her interest and attention persisted.
Serving me well to perform efficiently
Especially with tasks thought difficult.
My inner mentor Sister Theo guided me.

Personal growth groups were organized.
Corporate presentations were conducted.
Non-profit organizations were created.
Fund-raising activities were accomplished.

When my sensibilities are challenged by
Audacity to conduct unfamiliar projects,
I call on inner Theo resources for success
My activities seem Theophana influenced.

When attending seminars or symposia,
And asked about my greatest influence,
My immediate response is Sister Theo
And I am the first to get up to speak.

Theo reclaimed her maiden name of Buissle.
And reverted to day clothes and no wimple.
Satisfying our curiousity to see what lurked
Underneath the pristine crisp white dimple.

Her vibrant energy and cheerful demeanor,
Her goodness and unfailing humanness,
Attested to the indelible impressions
She made on her business associations.

She hoped she had served God well
To claim her place in His kingdom.
She lives forever in our hearts and minds,
Her Young Christian Students- YCS Girls.

***

Perception

He thought his family
was so wealthy.
He and his siblings
were well clothed,
well fed, well bred
and well spoken.
They did not want
for anything.
Associated with people
like themselves.
They did not know
the number of
sacrifices made by
their parents to
keep them in this
state of grace.

***

Second Chance

Which is more desirous, a second chance
Or to move towards a new lifestyle?
The answer is contained in the question
And requires some thoughtful probing.

Is there a greater appeal in a second chance
Or a move to a seemingly new life?
Do the making of fresh choices entail
Much effort from both involved parties?

A second chance may be better desired
For what the first chance did not deliver.
While embracing the familiar and known
And hoping to salvage the manageable.

If it had been manageable,
Why did the relationship break down?
How to amend and make it better?
Much will be required for success of
A second chance or a renewed life.

A second chance implies new behaviour.
Some may think they are reverting to
The current state of same old, same old.
And situations will get better if one party
Changes without much effort from the other.

A second chance may continue
As an improvement of current life.
An enticement to work towards
Addressing issues causing the rift,
And resolutions to move forward.

Working together to make this whole,
Hoping past experiences will hold
To inform the situation and cause
A reconciliation for a new chance.
Reconciliations require determination.

What would reconciliations require?
A call to self- awareness of both parties,
Is there empathy for another's feelings?
Is there understanding of the other?
Do they show respect and kind regards?

Is there agreement for goal setting?
Are aspirations accepted and dependable?
Is companionship desired in the relationship?
Can these be integrated in the second chance
For peace, enjoyment and contentment?

New life requires healing and forgiveness.
A mindset which renews the past and
Embraces blessings for a second chance.
A decision has to be made as to whether
It is desirous to go or start anew.

We all need second chances.
We make errors in judgement,
Careers, relationships and acquisitions.
We wish certain situations had not occurred
And hope for a second chance to repair.

When issues are honestly probed;
Failings fairly acknowledged;
Successes consciously celebrated;
Improvements willingly applied;
There is hope for a second chance.

A second chance integrates a new life
Allowing great learning limiting strife,
Willingness to work for great respite,
Cordial and interactive companionship,
To make for long-lasting relationship.

Where a second chance is improbable,
Differences are mainly irreconcilable;
Emotional damage deeply irreparable;
Workable alternatives inconceivable;
The new learning could benefit all.

As new learning informs a second chance,
So, it benefits moving to a new life.
Parties become aware of their shortcomings
Accept themselves and others as they are
And accept situations that currently exist.

Most are desirous of peace and happiness.
Peace is imbued in accepting the new life.
Happiness is infused in the second chance.
The new life and second chance are graced
By gratitude, love and wisdom of guidance.

***

True Confessions

True Confessions Magazines
Totally captivated my senses,
When I avidly read them
As a gullible teenager.
I was totally fascinated
By their riveting stories
Of unrequited love,
Unhappy love affairs
And ongoing heartbreak.
The stories seemed romantic.
The drama of it all excited my
Love-struck imagination.
Multiple love crushes had me
Dreaming of romantic
And happy ever-afters.
To keep the dreams alive,
I tried different types
Of loving in later years.
Unrequited love caused me
Heart-wrenching aches.
Unhappy love affairs gave
Me splitting headaches.
I was deliriously seeking
Out potential suitors
And pitting them against
Trivial dalliances.
I played hard ball and
The perpetual drama,
Drove me senseless.
My adventures could have
Been written on many
Newsstand magazines.
The daily tabloids embellish

Them with possible rumours.
Those dramas and romances
Constantly caused me aches.
None of my later loves
Could compensate
For those fanciful years,
Until You!
My True Confession.

***

Caution

Take out the trash bin
Without complaining,
But with a charming grin
And a cheerful good morning.

***

Please, Mom, cuddle me
On your beautiful chest.
So, I can suckle your nutritious breast
And let nature do the rest.

***

Take care of what is entrusted to you,
And be blessed with abundance.

***

Focus on what you desire to accomplish
And be successful.

***

Plant seeds of goodness in your very young
And watch them grow into beautiful people.

***

When you sow flower seeds in your little garden front
You will have blooming flowers.

***

If you do the same things repeatedly,
You will get the same results.

**

If thousands of words play in my brain,
I will have misspelling.

**

Inflexibility causes breakage from the whole
Too difficult to mend.

**

If you want something that is unavailable,
You must work harder to acquire it.

**

The outward appearance is not determinant
Of the inward intentions.

**

Patience and trust will reveal
That which is internally conceived.

**

Invoke the past for learning and growth
Not to bring back anger and pain.

**

Passing Away

So sad today:
So many friends
Are passing away.
And so many are
Getting ready to go.
I would have
Liked to have kept
You much longer,
But it is not up
To me, so I say
"God sped, my friends.
I well miss your
Laughter and smiles.
I will miss your
Wise council."
And hold on
Tightly, while
I command my
Soul that it is
Ordained rightly
To God's plan
For the better.
And console
My spirit to be of
Good cheer.
While you leave
The days bereft,

You are now
Distinctive stars
Which brighten
The nights
Awaiting our coming.

***

It's Okay

Poet Rumi's poem
"Don't go back
To sleep,"
Could mean,
Be alert and aware.
My Mum makes
A pronouncement
To "Take it Easy!"
When she wants
To prevent a feud
As she sees
Tensions rising.
I think most
Situations turn out
"Okay!"

The poet and my mum
already knew
Their reasonings
Were sound.
They had already
Learned to trust.
Trust takes a long
Time to come.
And has one wondering
Whether this or that
Would work and if not,
What would?

Pulling out old
Writings of decades ago,
And seeing that they
Seemed okay,

Thought I should
Revive my writing.
Not knowing how
To begin and not
Knowing what I will
Be saying,
Took a blank page.
Allowed trust to
Settle in my awareness,
Started the writing
While I say,
"It's okay!"

With trust, I feel
Confident to let go.
Surrender!
And allow myself
To be inspired.
Accept what comes,
Knowing that
It is all for the good.
And now say,
"It's okay!"

I hold on to trust
And it has not yet
Abandoned me.
Poetry writing
Has opened up
A long-awaited
Avenue of expression.
As I take the plunge
I am learning to trust
And say
"It's okay!"

In the days when
The poet's alert
And aware delude
Me and I become
Careless and
Clumsy, I forgive
Myself and say
"It's okay!"

When my Mum's
Tendre of taking
It easy is
Overlooked in
Favour of loud
Disagreements,
I pause and think
There must be
Another way of
Looking at this
And concede,
"It's okay!"

In indecisive
Moments, testing
Possible decisions
And outcomes,
I look and see what
Could be the best
Results based on my
Values, then leave
The decision-making to
Trust. Accept and say,
"It's okay!"

When things don't go
According to plan,
Despite my best efforts,
I acknowledge my
Disappointments,
Shrug my shoulders
and live to face
Another day, saying,
"It's okay!"

When misunderstood,
I wonder why this
Came about.
What happened
To invoke that response?
I reflect on what
Occurred, body
Language, tone of voice,
Facial expressions.
What brought it about?
Take responsibility for
My actions, then say,
"It's okay!"

Knowing that all
Is not perfect;
Knowing too,
That I can't have
All that I want;
But knowing that
life holds my
Best interest,
With my back-up
Of trust, I say,
"It's okay!"

When having
A decision under
Consideration,
After much deliberation,
My first option is
To trust that all
May be well. Then
Move with confidence
And acceptance;
Then surrender, saying,
"It's okay!"

Life continues with
Or without situations
Out-of-control.
To be alive is
To deal with the
Situations that
Come our way.
We may sometimes
Be alert and aware.
We may sometimes
Take it easy, and we may
Learn to trust and say,
"It's okay!"

The going sometimes
Gets rough.
Whether we are
Aware of its
Approach or not,
We inadvertently get
Caught in the crossfire.
When maligned,
Do what is

Possible to defuse
Or clear the situation
Then, let it go saying,
"It's okay!"

When alert and aware
Are neglected,
And Mum's easiness,
Is not exercised,
Something fails.
To reclaim my saving
grace, I invoke
Prayers of forgiveness
For the negligence.
And prayers of gratitude
For assistance received.
Then say,
"It's okay!"

Quiet Country Lane

Comfort

I was awoken
From this dream,
By a sudden
Movement of an
Elbow din.
A jab to push
Away the two hands
Creeping from behind
And holding me at my waist.
I was not sharing
My bed with anyone.
I did not invite anyone in.
Who had snuck into my bed
While I was fast asleep?
The touch startled me.
I suddenly awoke
And turned around
To see who it could be.
I felt cozy and warm,
I felt secure and loved,
Though I could see no one.
It was an angel hug,
An unexpected hug,
A hug of comfort.

Water Fowls and Young

The Absent Father

He had not expected such a responsibility.
She had taken his flirty dalliance seriously.
He was just sowing his young wild oats,
Had no intentions of making lasting oaths.
Had not anticipated his natural instincts
Would result in begetting a baby offspring.

Shirking responsibility was not his intention.
He needed to have paid much better attention
To what he should to avoid that eventuality.
He could not think with any reasonability
Except attribute to their mutual attraction
Which caused them momentary distraction.

This distraction was proving quite costly
To wrap their heads about what to do mostly
To appease the growing concerns of the other.
He asserted he did not have much to offer
And at this time could think of nothing better
Except that they carry on like little mattered.

There were few job opportunities at home
And much opening employment overseas.
Worthy occupation to provide a livelihood.
He was faced with making a major decision
To stay and be with his young family or go.
He then accepted the far-a-way employment.

Saw my dad on two occasions in my lifetime.
Once at age fourteen, then age twenty-seven.
But I knew he cared, for he sent me presents.

A beautiful watch hiding under long sleeves,
A tartan school bag, the only one in school.
Bikini swim wear, the only one on the island.

A brown leather purse which I still want today.
White granny shoes were the height of the day
And so many pens, pencils, cases and books.
Such beautiful gifts from a dad living overseas.
Despite his visits and gifts and joy in seeing him,
Could not bring myself to call him father or dad.

I know he cared and wished he could do more.
We cared he was absent to direct my chores,
To prepare for and celebrate my milestones,
To be proud of me and rejoice in my successes.
To comfort my failures and explain my errors.
We needed each other in loving and bonding.

I would have loved to have known him better.
Sat with him and talked with much laughter.
Enjoyed his music, swimming and riding,
And generous father daughter volunteering.
Can't tell what relationship we could have had,
Based on my observation of other family ties.

I never saw an enviable father child relationship.
Never saw a father playing with his daughter.
And had no reliable model to base my knowing.
Except to say fathers had a hard time relating,
In turn, they themselves had no role models
And could not give what they had not received.

When fathers were absent from children's lives,
It became difficult to find a family unit where
Parents were physically and emotionally present.

Some people grew up with that void of bonding.
A misunderstanding of important natural ruling,
A necessity for an empathetic love relating.

With growing awareness of our way of being,
Fathers are learning the importance of modelling,
And play a stronger role in children's mentoring,
Coaching, instructing, championing, sympathizing,
Aiding the nurturing and bonding with offspring.
As they grow closer with current mode of parenting.

Fathers are more involved in children's welfare,
Compensating for what they missed and never had.
They give attention to children's reading and breeding,
Helping the moms with their grooming and feeding.
They are the dads whom we wish we had had,
Present, loving and helpful when most needed,
Hoping to be a less absent father than their own.

***

Time Revealed

What is this deliberate separating
Of time components,
Dividing remembrances
Of today, tomorrow and yesteryear?

***

What is this incessant chattering,
Wild crazy imaginings
Never actualized
In today's reckoning?

***

What is this constant recollecting
Regrets and issues,
Too inconsequential of
A past best forgotten?

***

What is this tedious losing
Of senseless mind games
And roller-coaster playing?
There is never much to gain!

***

What is this obtuse pronouncement
Discontent and disagreement
With all, whilst
Proclaiming your utter happiness?

***

What is this sacramental forgiving
Collectively administered,
Coincidently seen in the dream
And in next morning's liturgy?

***

What is this perpetual hankering
After a brutal past
And a set of painful sentiments
Repugnant at the time of happening!

***

What is this threatened prancing,
Like a professional boxer
Waving belligerent fists
Preparing for a fight?

***

What is this sly sneaking
Of determined aggression
A body-mind sensation,
Moving through the crowd?

***

What is this pained disparaging
Fear of the devastation,
Thinking all is lost?
When this too, shall pass!

***

What is this vulnerable crying,
That a busy brother
Is unloving
For his delay in returning a call?

***

What is this fragile rejecting
As a self-absorbed snob,
A neighbour preoccupied
With his own concerns?

***

What is this intimate cuddling
Of glorious splendour,
During a blissful night
Wrapped in the arms of the deity?

***

Aloneness

Through this long solemn road,
I walk alone, unperturbed and
Undisturbed.

Seeking out as companions, nature's
Sights and sounds of its many
Creatures.

Its sights are wonderous to behold
Complimenting the feel of awesome
Beauty.

Its sounds are harmonious and
Blend invitingly with my mood of
Aloneness.

I feel at one with them all and
My lively steps appreciatively fall
In sync.

Alone, I wonder what is loneliness?
What is the feeling and is it felt only when
Alone?

Lonely may occur alone or otherwise.
Loneliness may set in when the mind
Is unwise.

A Wandering of mind to bring back past
Memories creating futile longing and
Emptiness.

Empty feelings that something is amiss
And needs to be filled by something or
Someone.

Sometimes the one thing most desirous
Does not occur and leaves that space
Void.

Sometimes the desire to be part of a crowd
Is so strong that a feeling of inadequacy
Persists.

Sometimes the one person wanted around
Is emotionally unavailable or absent creating
A loss.

If this something or someone is not present
At the moment, this emptiness persists as
Insufficiency.

Feelings of inadequacy make believe that
You and your accomplishments are not
Enough.

When will all that is needed, be enough?
When will sufficiency fill up all time and
Space?

This space may temporarily be filled by
Interesting activities, beautiful objects and
Thoughts.

When thoughts are focused on wanting, the
Unavailable and unattainable give rise to
Loneliness.

Loneliness is an emptiness searching of
An external outlet to obliterate the nagging
Longing.

This longing can be mitigated in part by
Focusing on the issues at hand and being
Attentive.

And in part, by learning to appreciate and
Utilize alone time for practising graces for
Posterity.

Invoking graces can lead to prosperity,
Deeping in the universal pool for ideas of
Creativity.

Creation is the divine source ever ready
To fill up the empty space with worthy
Activities.

Activities, well intentioned, large or small
Will defray the onslaught of feelings of
Inadequacy.

Aloneness is necessary to incubate thoughts
And ideas and bring them to fruition as active
Participation.

Participation dispels the feeling of loneliness,
When creativity has already been conceived in
Aloneness.

***

Roasted Ground Beans

(Grandmothers)

A pungent smell whiffed the air,
Of ground roasted coffee fare,
So familiar throughout the year.
I sniffed the aroma of the grind,
Bringing nostalgia so defined
By my deep tender past.

Roasted coffee brought to mind,
My grandmothers on both sides.
Fully engaged in separating rind,
A grandma called Mama Eggit,
Grandma Mary called my granny.
Of my deep tender past.

Fun to use the quaint coffee mill
To grind the coffee beans therein,
While bickering to see who will win
The game of sucking sweet cacao seeds,
Before putting in the roasting bin
In our deep tender past.

The roasting bin fired by roaring coals
Was tended by our Grandma Eggit
As we playfully assessed the final goals.
First the coffee beans were roasted,
Then the cocoa seeds were toasted.
In the deep tender past.

One granny did all the roasting.
The other did the cocoa grinding
While we wished to do all the minding.
Both grandmas ground beans tending
Coffee milling, cocoa stick rolling.
In our deep tender past.

Mama Eggit soothed our aches.
She prepared our daily takes
And forgave silly mistakes.
She roasted the dried cocoa beans
And ground roasted coffee beans
In our deep tender past.

Mama Eggit directed our chores.
She kept us well-fed and well-washed.
And a weekly exchange of library books.
School holidays were a great adventure
Which took us all over the Island blast
Of our deep tender past.

Mama extended goodwill and kindness.
Lunchtime to share expansive rations,
As though chosen to care for the nation,
She succoured many visiting drop-ins,
Listening and giving good old counsel,
In our deep tender past.

Persons came by visiting regularly.
In awe, we wondered who they could be!
How did she know from where they came?
Some were rural relatives staying overnight
As we curiously followed their oversights
In our deep tender past.

Granny Mary reserved our spots
Protecting us from rushes and roughs.
As we hide from the carnival drops
From the revelling bands and din
Coming down Constitution Hill.
In our deep tender past.

Granny Mary was a candy maker.
She crafted fudges, lollipops and takers,
Delighting kids on the way to school.
Satisfying the ready sweet drool.
Transforming fruits into jellies and jams
In my deep tender past.

With treats, sweets and loving care,
Dreaming of all the goodies to share,
Grannies made days especially dear.
Waking to morning coffee brew,
Ending the night with our cocoa drew.
In our deep tender past.

Grandmas performed caring rituals,
From tasks of roasting and the grind
To charming people from all around.
Quite fortunate to have had two grandmas
Preparing our favourite beverage kinds.
In our deep tender past.

Mortar & Pestle & Grinder

Old Age

A Flashing smile brightened his wrinkled face.
Wrinkles that spoke of whom and what he's been
And a face revealing decades of gracious living.

He made an effort to go outside the home
To sit on the bench under the noonday sun.
And warm and sooth his old aching bones.

His old sweetheart was coming by to chat.
The one who seemed closer to his heart,
Continuing an affair which did long ago start.

Smiles widely peeping through deep folds,
That special greeting for him only told.
As she slowly approached in a walking chair.

They returned smiles and cheerful greetings.
A good day with no pains urged them on
To reminisce about those days long gone.

He had caused her much heartache when
He flaunted about with youthful prowess
Thinking himself irresistible to the lioness.

Despite the teasing about his early conquests,
Sparks still crackled between those two.
Who knew such attraction would ever last?

"You still care," He cowry chided her.
"Had better in case you do not wake next year.
"Just saying I love you as my neighbour."

"Charming old girl," He was heard to mutter.
"Imagine her thinking we will not go together.
"We have spent a lifetime knowing each other."

A litany of on-again, off-again careless courting,
Not a moment in time, she could say he is mine.
That always refuted his declarations of loving.

How she suffered through his sowing wild oats.
Surprised it mattered and she truly hurt.
Could not convince him that she really cared.

This lasted for too long, she wouldn't leave.
Each time he pleaded, "hang in there and stay!"
Until taking courage, she left one day.

Her new love excited a better way.
But thoughts of their loving never went away
Forever intruding with reminders array.

Did not expect the love to last that long.
Discovered through her many furloughs,
Her love grew with the passage of time.

Here we are again, having come full circle.
Unsure if I'll see you again and the morrow
Knowing that our love survived the hallow.

I experienced much struggles on the way.
Thinking I could achieve with continuous play.
Until children came along to change the sway.

Had one failed marriage, attempted another.
Have four children, seven grand children
And three great grand who keep me enthralled.

I have since lost my wife, but I now live
To hear my children's laughter and vibes,
Having them near for cheerful contrive.

Unable to say a full coherent sentence,
My friend forgets the words she wants
And grapples with dismal memory loss.

Angry about her increasing memory loss,
In childish tantrums throw objects about
Until her frustration gradually stops.

Last night he said good bye to Buddy
In his final days and didn't expect to last.
All his children now gone and no one to pass.

Buddy had been an entrepreneur spending
Too much time working and none playing.
His life ended alone with no more swaying

But their time together was becoming rarer.
Each day saw them older and friends scarcer.
The group was fast dwindling and sparser.

So happy to be spending time together.
His aches spike up sometimes, but not today.
Being with her is so very exciting and gay.

They continued to speak of youthful times,
When they lived for the coming party limes,
Teasing and jeering at old passers-by.

Little did they know their time would come,
When they would be seen in wheel chairs
And no longer fast cars with loud mufflers.

Well, my dear, we've lived a full life,
Destined as sorrow and pain and joy
And happiness which we still share now.

***

My Mother

A new baby girl born to a child.
A mere child with no middle name,
A constant reminder that she came,
A surprise and a welcomed addition
To a vibrantly robust house of seven.
She was the sixth sibling and last
Replacing one of twins long passed.

A child coupling with another
Talented, handsome and popular.
A teenager whose charming style
She could only sometimes resist.
He played the trumpet like no other.
Great in their class, they discovered.
The pull of undeniable attraction
Propelling them closer together.

Just children in growing puberty,
Having feelings strange and tingly
All so peculiar and frightening,
Too intimate for open happening.
In a culture where most was secret,
Children should be seen not heard.
Nothing explained, little learned.
Left them alone to their exploring.

Parental closeness so long denied,
Touch only to sooth minor cries.
Kissing with only privileged few
Rendering hugging purely defiled.

No wonder their lively curiosity,
Struggling with the bloom of love,
Their need for comfort and sharing
Caused tentative forbidden playing.

One encounter, hesitant for others,
Thoughtful suspects of love uncertain.
Her swelling body soon confirmed
An expectant child shamed to a mother.
Herself, a multiplier of woes because
Of spouse's carousing and infidelities.
Hopes and dreams of a daughter's future
Dashed at becoming a school teacher.

Determined to gain respectability,
Her choice of occupation, shopkeeping.
Employment reserved for relatives mostly.
Re-awakening hormones two years later
Attracted yet another tall debonair.
He desired to make a permanent union,
A notion flatly rejected and denied
But found herself again with child.

Now a youth with adult obligations,
Her mainstay remained shopkeeping.
Two girls, her only living offspring.
She shared caring for her two nieces
Whose parents immigrated overseas.
And lamented that her beloved Dad
Talented and skilled neglected to add
Opportunities better for family living.

Her duties were discharged reverently
Ensuring our school attendance daily
And Sunday school and Mass weekly.

She took pleasure in dressing her girls
Infusing in them her sense of style
Basking in attention paid by all
To their dazzling looks and clever zeal
Showing off deportment and grace.

Our entire education occupied her mind,
Furthering our learning in private time,
Joining events with Brownies and Guides
And crafting objects from crochet and ties.
Her pride came in play when we annually
Received awards for excellence efficiency.
We always featured in drama and plays
Delighting neighbours with joyous ways.

Family concerts were our absolute joy.
She taught us poetry, song and dance.
Today, we marvel that a girl so young
Had knowledge and wisdom entranced.
She quoted Shakespeare, Milton and things.
Sang Gregorian Latin chants and hymns.
Had won popular singing competitions
And graciously danced the current swing.

Endowed with her dad's music and song,
Delivered her singing with charm and wit.
Entertaining her many diverse friends
With flashing smiles and beautiful tweets.
Often times, her visiting friends were
Fashionable ladies and young men
And Catholic priests and stevedores.
She gave listening ear to many neighbours.

Her happiness continued to ring out,
In her tenor octaves teasing voice,
Convincing all she was a singing man.
My greatest delight was time spent
While she practised the Latin Mass;
Sang school songs and current pop.
I tried to emulate that lovely voice
With tongue-in-cheek and no success.

Her generosity knew no bounds.
Sharing Sunday meals with the homeless,
Making sure we extended gentleness.
Awarding little jobs to fix this and that
To fulfill one of her acts of charity.
Donating in measure to church and cause.
Her debtors never forgot her kindness
And even today try to make recompense.

She eventually chose a husband.
The household became quiet and still.
There were no quarrels to remember.
Gentle teasing was the order of the day.
A union apparently loving and gay
But undermined by frequent failings
Of dubious fidelities and secret play.
A fate discouraged for her daughters.

Her love for us pronounced in words,
"I'll go to hell for my children!"
Unfortunately came close to the truth
As reaching the brink of hell's gate,
Was hauled back by an act of faith,
And trust in God's forgiving grace.
Life continued evenly until we moved
And her sister reclaimed her charges.

The quiet and silence prevailed,
Broken only by her daily therapy
Of sitting to launder and verbally
Replay misfortunes of the day;
A carry over from other times
When her days were not going fine.
Listening to her affected me greatly,
As she required much sympathy.

Her joy was greatly expressed
With her children's pleasures and tests,
And her relatives' triumphs and wins.
Her greatest release was at carnival limes,
Her days for shedding trials and whines.
With her sisters, some rum grog and wine,
Put her in spirit for some glorious while,
To be repeated next year at the same time.

Like a mother hen, she shielded her own.
A mother's need to protect her young,
Did not prevent us from doing wrong.
No matter how reverent her attempts,
Our ultimate goal to seek and discover.
Often, knowing her abject vulnerability,
We changed courses to soften the blow.
But life's teachings, we could not forgo.

Blessed with much knowledge and smarts,
She was well read, well spoken and bright.
Conferring with presidents, doctors and priests
Who stopped at her shop for a little chit chat,
About community, spirituality and politics.
She spoke with authority and confidence
Unafraid to voice her opinions and her truths.
A treasure to her organization and groups.

Her personality was strong and flexible,
Her character made an impression indelible.
She extended kindness and goodwill,
Dispelled anger, sloth and ill will.
She instilled in us love for song and dance
And an interest in learning and growing.
Some say she was a giant woman.
Some say she was the nicest human.

The young have never heard her voice.
I have heard no other like hers.
There is much more that can be said
But this medium is not conducive to
Capturing her entire essence and such.
She was more than those few words.
A private woman without gossip nor guile
Full of goodness, kindness and charm.

Your mother may be similar to her,
With abounding courage and strength.
A very special breed facing adversity
To support their children's travesty.
Their children, their pride, pain and joy.
Their devotion to God and prayer
See them through trials and fear.
This is my tribute to the mothers of all.

Each mother is special to her own.
A choice made for us to acknowledge
And revere a mother so loving and caring.
A mother like no other was my mother.

Whom we all called Tanty, others, Lucy.
Others called her Ma Grell or Mrs. Grell
Forever will dwell in my heart and mind
Until we join again in the next lifetime

***

Mistakes

The family gathering was a commotion.
An argument of what was right or wrong,
A situation requiring a determination.
The family thought a mistake was eminent.
But the decision maker was adamant,
Could not be persuaded to change her mind.
Some saw signs and could not deny
There would be drawbacks down the line.

The debate was temporarily resolved
As the perpetrator took responsibility
For the outcome of her conscious acts.
She was of the opinion that all was well,
The results would be just as her foretell.
A great adventure with a successful end.
After all was said and done, the portend
Unanticipated, disastrous and undesired.

This disaster was called a big mistake,
Citing some unintended limitations
That could not deliver the expectations.
But it is said, one learns by one's mistakes.
How many must be conceived and delivered
To be convinced that indeed mistakes are
A learning tool happening in hindsight?
Recognized only when the deed was done?

So many mistakes are made and are called
A mishap when the cooking pot boils over;
An error when the opposite direction
Is taken from what was described;
An accident when my foot hits a curb
And I fall prone in a sidewalk ditch;

A miscalculation of the musical scores
Rendering the music piece out of pitch.

They can be called by name, mis-takes,
When an offering is accidentally missed;
Preferring the least expected to succeed;
And opportunities remain ignored by
Careless consideration of possibilities.
Mistakes occur when we are not mindful;
Tend to thoughtlessly shape our decisions.
And may cause a wave of incompletions.

Some mistakes may be trivial and insular,
Like our tone of voice and bad manners,
And how we treat ourselves and others.
Some are huge and make a big difference
Like the storming of the French Bastille;
Airplane crash destroying all mercantile.
Mistakes may be costly and sometimes fatal
And should be avoided at all times.

When mistakes occur, some express regrets.
Had I known, I shoulda, coulda, woulda.
Some eventualities could be mistakes
And may be considered learning tools.
When undesirable results occur despite
Careful planning and realistic expectations
And results do not turn out as planned,
They are then renounced as mistakes.

A mistake happens by carelessness.
And may be avoided by mindfulness
Applying your values to make choices;
Praying for wisdom in your execution;
Forgiving mishaps and missed graces.

Giving full focus to your where with all,
Noting well directions given and taken.
Watching where you tread to break the fall.

Balancing accounts to avoid over spends.
To all accounts, it all comes down to now.
Paying attention to the here and now.
Being in the present moment to grasp all.
Living in mindfulness of all and now
To avoid mishaps, errors, miscalculations.
Everything happens in attention to the now
And a focus to learn by our mistakes.

***

The Romantic Soul

The romantic soul yearns for lovers,
Preoccupied with the wanting and having,
Who have forgotten about the giving and being,
Who misunderstand the art of living.

The romantic soul wants to breath
Joy and happiness in their loving embrace.
But lovers can scarcely be found.
They hide among the material
Chasing after the more.

The soul wants to bring back
That loving feeling,
The tenderness, the touch, the longing,
The look that says, "I love you!"
The love which sets the spirit free
To express grandly;
And keeps the soul enthralled
In its doings purposefully.

***

Memory

When a thought enters your head,
Hold and repeat it until it is read.
Drop what you are doing and
Reach for paper and pen.
Quickly write down the thoughts,
Lest they elude you and go in
Hibernation until another time.

The elusive thought pops up again
Looking for the original
Place it once occupied.
Not finding it, settles in a new spot
Where it no longer fits.

The misplaced thought,
Coming at odd uncalled times,
Suggests to those around
You are probably no longer with it.
And should be treated with gentle
Reservation or committed
To a correctional institution.

What has happened to that
Agile brain that it no longer
Works as well as it did?
We need to be continuously
Digging in and plodding
The mind to get the words
To say what we mean.

Mind sometimes in turmoil,
Wishing to be more this,
Longing for the other that.

Seldom at peace.
Always searching,
Wanting, seeking, praying,
Getting, discarding, inviting,
Doing, all in busy accord.
Inventing unlikely scenarios.
Throwing the memory in chaos.

Chaos exists when the brain
Is unequally employed.
The left side does not know
What the right is doing and
Feels unequally loved,
Causing trans circuit fighting
With memory caught in
The middle of the cross fire.
Sending minute cells into hiding
In spatial lapses of timing.

Memory keeps slipping back
To forbidden territory and
Provokes events best forgotten.
Always preventing us from
Living in the valuable now.

Memory conjures images
Of fantasies and
Unrealistic expectations,
Leading to disappointments
And broken promises.
Obscuring the eternal moments.

Mind tricks obscure the memory
Causing a play on names and places.
Which cannot recall in good order

A given name to a specific face;
Identify a described space;
Remember a mentioned name;
But later settles and puts them together.

When needed words are forgotten,
Blank spaces are left on the screen,
Or the sentence is kept hanging
Waiting for a sudden revelation.
Memory later kicks in, and
Fills the space with the right words,
Fulfilling the requirements.
Memory is kind and eventually
Brings all needed words together.

Spontaneity, the required result;
Freedom, the ultimate goal;
Happiness, the connecting factor;
If only we could come by these
Without struggle and strain!

Keeping the brain agile
And the memory in the present
Require specific conditions,
Peace of mind and meditation,
Intervening laughter and play,
A healthy dose of food for thought
And constant maintenance to
Keep it loving, receiving and giving.

***

Creole *(Kwéyòl)*

A culture abolishing its enslaved past
Exudes its beauty that forever last.
A creole woman with hands on her hips,
Basket perched jauntily on head tips,
Tell a tale of independence and grief.

Independence to give bold, glowing vent,
Freedom in expressions and movements,
Melding touches of Europe, Asia, Africa,
Emerging as celebrations in the Americas.
Escaping some grief from a colonial era.

Proudly, she stands without apology.
Unwilling to dispose of her liberty
To pose, compose, impose and expose
Joy in her selfness as she laughs loudly,
Caressing her attractive hips seductively.

Les Creoles prepare for celebrations,
With beginnings already in full oblation.
Seizing hand-down rites from generations,
Compositions evolving with inventions.
Revelries continuing without demotions.

Compositions exuberant in preparation,
Hailed from ancient decrees and fashions.
Styles preserved for specific occasions,
Every mode has its space, time and place.
Fashioned so all could enjoy their grace.

Inventions extravagant in their rendering,
No stopping the vibrant wild imaginings,
Bringing out all dormant meanderings,

Laying bear antiquity to creole sightings
A tapestry of old-world charm merging.

The creole woman enjoys admiration
When she poses on Sundays and special times,
Walking gracefully on the land, fan in hand,
On her way to church as neighbours stand
Staring at a sight too beautiful to understand.

She wears her colourful *Wòb dwiyèt,*
Starched layered petticoats *san sigwète.*
Requiring much of church pew to l*adjé,*
Drawing attention to elegant *tètkassé*
Gold *ponm kanèl* and stylish filigree.

Festivals are kept joyous with deals,
Food preparations for delicious meals.
Un bonm kalalou et koubouyon pwéson
A fusion of seafoods and provisions.
Paired with intensified rum grog punch.

Festivals continue under mango trees,
Where spirited *jing-ping* bands tease.
Accordion and *chakchak* rattle *gwaj,*
Stomping beat of the *boumboum* rap.
Enticing all to dance to drums and tap.

Bèlè has begun, a popular dance of the day.
Bare foot works in time with drums and l*avwé.*
A dance of freedom, flirting, courting and play.
Fast moves challenging to the naked eye.
Furious steps jump agilely from left to right.

Drums play to feet. Feet sing to music.
Music and dance speak *kwéyòl,*
Steps and sounds play in sync.
Fast and furious the festival come in high swing,
Dancing, spinning, twirling, whirling, swirling.

Different styles of dance continue in *souks.*
Dances of *quadrille, bèlè soté, mazouk,*
Enjoyed by women dressed in madras *jip.*
Men swaggering in black, white and red.
Fashions modernized from colonial threads.

The community *bèlè* singers chant l*avwé*
Of a second chance for missed opportunities,
The ongoing conversations of creole festivities.
As dancers magically make their pleas,
With movements of flirting, seducing a tease,

Natives are unimpeded to speak *patois,*
A dialect interjecting many conversations,
As assertions of curiousity and dissentions,
As a seductive invitation to all expressions.
Passionate in its cadence and exclamations.

Creole expressions of oms, ahs and ees,
Like ancient Sanskrit reverberating the hills,
Can take aggressive turns when peeved,
Spewing out imaginative cussing words
To gentle discerning ears better unheard.

Rhythmic tones harmonize the dialect,
Patwa spoken as first or second elect.
Music to the ears like sacred devotions,
expressing a multitude of deep emotions.
Speech, language and tongue in celebration.

Festivals build remarkable togetherness.
Returning Islanders, visitors and patriots,
Smiles of happiness spread like chariots.
Enchanted by country air, mountains and sea.
Delighted by all they hear, fancy and see.

Streets and markets festooned with gaiety.
Pretty merchandising stalls vie for beauty.
Captivating songs, music and dance lure
Women in beautiful imitations of *wob*,
Swaying to *lapo kabrit* and *jing-ping* bob.

Celebrating visitors enjoy blessed time
Relinquishing trials and enlivening ties.
Glorious days for neighbours and friends
Sharing blessings, love, goodwill, and charm.
Events sanctified by churches throughout.

A joyous culture is a profound inheritance
Of celebrations, rejuvenation and repatriation.
The culture is domestic, stylistic and creative,
A bonding of customs, values and lives.
Creole is the celebration of cultural festivities.

Creole Women

(L-R) Ziska White, Deborah Gage, Lorraine Dorival, Germaine Rabess, Gillian Alleyne, Antoinette Charles-Owen, Connie Alleyne, Jennifer White, Lyn White.

Birds

One morning, they came making a racket,
Cooing, cahing, calling, fluttering packets.
Just being happy while bringing some news
Flying free, playfully admiring the views.

They bring me news of life's passing
While I look for them to pass the day.
But they have not been around for a while,
And it was not even yet winter time.

Missed you, thinking you had gone south.
Then, saw you frolicking on the neighbour's porch.
Where have you been, fine feathered friends?
Thought you deserted me, another to befriend.

With your partner, you took flight.
Well chosen your partner for life.
Like loving couples, never leaves your sight,
Freedom in your flight, harmony in your sighs.

You teased with deep-throated cries,
'There was no need to worry at all.
We were just playing with friends and all
And would come back to tell all was well.'

All day they played chasing each other,
Cooing and cahing and singing together.
Flying off with friends who passed by, but
Coming back to rest in their favorite bower.

They choose a sleeping place that night,
On the balcony marked by their right.
A familiar place littered with droppings
A comfort to them from nightly prowlings.

Saw the black bird standing like a willow,
Awaiting the mate's return at the window.
Wondered whether her patience was waring,
As she anxiously continued her pacing.

All seemed well when next I looked.
They were sitting comfortably beak to beak.
Giving a show of gentle companionship,
And a look of forgiving friendship.

Hypnotized by their every move,
Saw them part ways, giving each a space.
Each sleeping a little distance apace
Allowing each a good night's respite.

They sang out bidding good morning
Remaining together for good bonding.
Maybe they are among the flocks around,
Flying high, singing there, feeding everywhere.

Many feathered friends are flying around.
Not easy to tell which ones you are abound.
You seem alike and behave as renowned.
Unless you separate, you will never be known.

Some are feeding from the sodden.
The green grass provides perfect fodder.
You peck in unison at tidbits unseen
Buried deep in the growing grass green.

Are you two of those feeding birdies?
Black and white plumes with iridescent green,
Forming a carpet of impenetrable bonding,
That no one dare approach and stake claim?

Would have liked to adopt you as my own,
But your bonds are tight as you move as one,
Starting, stopping, flying and pecking to order
From a particular cue given by the leader.

Which is that special leader you obey?
You all seem obedient and happy to comply.
You just open, spread your wings and fly.
Freedom for a while until next feeding time.

Story of the birds is not complete.
Spotted two mates with five baby chicks.
Strolling and pecking on the grounds.
Were they the love birds with their young?

They have the mating art to a science.
Giving signals of general acquiescence.
Like kindred spirits learning and playing
Teaching sessions wherever they're staying.

They follow the lessens of the teacher
Also obey the cues given by their leader.
They show companionship and togetherness
While exercising patience and forgiveness.

The birds have flown away for awhile.
Playfully scampering around for miles.
Are they learning to impart their wisdom,
Growing, feeding, existing in the now?

***

Credo

We believe that:-

Life which was given to us is our greatest asset
To be shared, fully appreciated,
Cherished and celebrated.
And we want you to believe that too.

You want to make some movement in that life.
You have dreams and goals and aspirations
To discover and explore.
You can attract all the resources you need to do so.
And we want you to believe that too.

You are multiple talented.
And it is your right to express those talents
Authentically and creatively.
And we want you to believe that too.

You have within you the answers to make
Your life more enjoyable,
Create what you want to make it more fulfilling.
And we want you to believe that too.

You are deserving of good health, wealth,
Love, happiness and success.
And we want you to believe that too.

You are creative, resourceful and whole
You want to believe in yourself.
There is no better time than now.
And we want you to believe that too.

***

The Hurricane

I approached the treacherous hilltop mound,
Carving out a little clearing from around
To allow a walkway for news and views
Where hurricane wreckage and rubble abound.

Everything laid bare for me to see.
Refuting all doubts that they did exist.
All conceivable objects around my feet
Now converted into substances defeat.

Bedsteads lost serviceable mattresses.
Frames twisted into pliable distresses.
Beddings shredded for patchwork quilts,
Will now serve purposes unintended.

A saucepan contorted into sculptural art,
Articles of clothing used for diverse parts,
Paintings of renowned artists unrecognizable,
Now strewn around to be noticeable.

What were mountains of lush forest greens,
Now completely flattened to the ground.
Trees, branches and boughs from the bend
Allowing vistas from one end to end.

Boulders unearthed by uprooted trees
Formed a guard with sarsens and twigs,
Protecting shrubs laying low on the wing
Unmoved by water and howling wind.

Skeleton house frames, roofless tops,
Welcomed fluttering birds, homeless
Like human friends, looking for a place
To rest and regroup, another day to face.

All that remained of the mango tree
Was a skeleton shredded and bleached.
While its earlier abundance of fruits
Was crushed by flying tempestuous things.

Flying things danced in blowing wind.
Refrigerators escaping doorless kitchens,
Swirled with one-legged chairs and table tops.
A choreography directed by curtain rods.

Mud slides came down from forest heights.
Mountains desecrated landings and sights,
Making bridges uncrossable, roads impassable.
All wondering where to turn, what's available?

Security shelters had been long designated.
Whereabouts completely now undetected.
Most buildings are totally empty shells.
Difficult to determine what is gone or held.

What was once a street is now a lake.
Running streams claimed walking trails.
Angry rivers gobbled by greedy waves.
Bridges merged with giant waterways.

A skinny dog reluctantly approached me.
Looking lost, distrustful and desolate
Like his last home which stands no more.
Gloomy as the lonely terrain, now so bare.

Uncomprehending in his look for love.
Disbelieving what has just occurred.
What has happened to his family and home?
Would he understand if explained to him?

Family cottage perched on the river's edge,
Its occupants feeling safe secure within.
Suddenly, the river erupted unapologetically
Carrying down everything that could be seen.

Family and cottage suffered a cruel fate.
So destructive that no one could be saved.
The river, in fury and rage grabbed all,
Cottage, rusted vehicles, persons and all.

Inhabitants of cottages were washed away
Ending who knows where, never seen again.
Rusted vehicles standing sentinel for decades
Relocated to where such things land to decay.

My family had experienced three miracles.
Evoking emotional tears when relayed.
One story was about the house rooftop leaks,
Still able to accommodate many of the sick.

The homeless told gruelling tales of terror,
Horror of raging winds and tumultuous downpours.
Miraculous escapades from dangerous targets,
And gratitude to God for seeing yet another day.

Teenagers ingeniously created a contraption
With a small school eraser and rubber band
Forming a wrench to hold a broken door.
The false latch kept them safe and secure.

Mama Eggit stood in her kitchen doorway,
Praying while she watched the angry fray.
Her grandchildren hurdled cozily indoors
Afraid of the monstrosity playing outdoors.

The monstrosity felled branches and trees
Coming to rest on rooftops and streets.
Mama Eggit saw the mango tree sway
Ready to crash mercilessly on stays.

With the reverence in her heart, she prayed,
As the tree bent towards a neighbour's yard.
The wind changed course, gusting furiously.
She continued to pray, much harder than last.

All seemed quietly calm as the wind subsided.
Thought her supplications had been ridded.
The danger had now passed and all was well.
But the hurricane was intent on causing ill will.

Suddenly, as if a thousand devils were pushing,
The mango tree shifted to fall on our kitchen.
An incident sure to cause loss of lives or limbs
Of distressed children hurdling from within.

Mama Eggit made a loud passionate plea
Calling for help needed from the deity.
She raised her hands to the heavens crying
For saving grace and our safeguarding.

She braced her strength against the wind.
Rain-drenched face, impassioned weeping,
Implored God's grace and his angels' help.
Faith and hope for her children's keeping.

"Not on my children!" she entreated.
Thereupon, saw the wind change course.
Tree ready to fall on a neighbour's house,
Suddenly changed uncertain trajectory.

Fervently she continued heartfelt requests.
Saw the tree fall snuggly between two decks,
Damaging one corner of a verandah porch,
While sparing lives and limbs of all about.

Tales of miracles and miseries interchangeably
Spoke of how nature manifested mysteriously,
The reverence of prayer, asking and receiving
And kindness and resilience of the human spirit.

Hurricane Remains

Myths and Legends.

A gargle of persons scattered the yard.
Curious neighbours standing, staring.
They heard she had not transformed
From her nightly flight as a witch
To her everyday look as a human.

We didn't know her given name.
She was never called by any one.
Only referred to as the *soucouyant.*
She never stopped to talk to anyone
And nobody ever dared speak to her.

Everyday she walked on the street,
Selfishly hogging the latrine stall.
No one came close to her at all.
Daily we stared at her cemetery crawl
As she walked against the dirty wall.

We wondered about her body parts.
Were they just like ours - humans?
She wore a soiled apron on her dirty dress.
Both of which had not been in a
Washing tub or pool of water for years.

Daily she left for parts unknown.
Was she one weeding the sidewalks?
Nightly when no one was around,
She fetched water with her butter tin
From public water taps by the gardens.

She lived in a shack in the yard.
No one dared go close to her abode.
One day, in my childish curiosity,

I peeped into her open doorway.
Saw what she had and how she lived.

Saw a collection of sticks and stones,
Dented cups, cracked plates and tins,
No bed, where did she sleep?
No chairs, where did she sit?
She will always remain a mystery.

She bought some oil from Ma John,
The only time I came close to her.
I strained to hear how she sounded.
She muttered so softly could not
Tell what language was lauded.

Poor old woman with no family,
No friends, the Roseau *soucouyant.*
We were not unkind, just fearful.
We could not tease her lest she
Came to suck our blood at nights.

What had happened that morning
To draw so many people to her yard.
Were they willing to help her?
Or just so full of curiosity,
Inquisitively following her movements?

Spectators whispered fearfully.
She had been pricked while flying,
Was ill and had difficulties changing
From nightly witch to a daytime person.
We never knew who she was.

***

I cuddled under my covers in bed.
My bedroom window overlooked the road.
I listened for the clanging of chains.
An indication that the *loogaroo*
Was close by coming for me.

Under a moody waning moon and
A shadowy night of moving clouds,
We were told the gruelling story of
The man with horse's legs and head
And bearing a human torso and arms.

He would be passing later that night.
And when we hear his clanging chains
We should take cover, less he comes
To get those who slept close to the road.
I listened all night for the clanging sound.

I intermittently covered and uncovered
My head when I sensed a movement.
I wanted to see. I was afraid to look.
Wanted to change places with my siblings
And have the *loogaroo* take them instead.

No! I could not let that happen.
I always protected my siblings.
I should take the hit instead.
I worked myself up to a frenzy.
Closed my eyes. Then, opened my eyes.
Couldn't sleep. Remained wide awake.
I waited all night but the *loogaroo* never came.

***

He is careful when walking the cemetery grounds,
Not to step on the graveyard dead.
And risk those buried pulling his legs
And take him down to be buried with them.

***

My siblings are all very strong swimmers. Not me!
Did not want to swim with my head under water
For fear *Laligne* would haul me to Canal Martinique.
I would miss my family and friends.

***

I watch her standing in six inches
Of water in the Roseau-river.
She thought the gentle flowing water
Was a major tidal wave ready to engulf her.
She just stood in the tiny pool and
Bawled her head out. Cried her eyes out.
Sobbing heartbrokenly that she was drowning.

***

The New City 2020

Wished to be in the old city mews
Walking on side walks, admiring the views,
Colonial houses with verandahs and pews
Most belonging to a privileged few.

Delighted to visit on those special dates,
Godmothers, family and school mates
After mass and casual times to droop
On their verandahs and in their stoops.

Such a tease to gaze in wonder
At families sitting down to dinner,
Clanking forks, knives and cutlery
Inviting passers-by to hear and see.

A lone girl sitting on a piano stool
Impelled by a driven anxious drool
To hit the keys, play out a tune
And so, impress her competitive clones.

The new city now boasts busy sidewalks
Occupied by harried traders and such,
Who jolt, cajole and patrol pavements
Impeding all comfortable movements.

Can hardly tell where I am going.
Vehicles line up streets on both sides
Blocking all views, passages and rides.
Rendering the place totally unrecognized.

The city façade is quickly changing.
The place is now unfamiliar ground.
Vendors have exhausted store premises
Using sidewalks to display their promises.

Fast honking cars, disgruntled patrons,
Walkways amass with merchandise
"A sign of progressive times", they say.
A sign of a developing nation today.

Returning patriots nostalgic for what
Was a genteel town of grace and droughts,
Long to see a semblance of old times;
Moving on comfortable rails and lines.

They long to browse in open store fronts;
Stop for a chat with old school comrades.
Stroll through uncluttered road ways.
Nonchalant and confident like old days.

Visiting patriots now seek refuge
In seaside, hillsides, mountain retreats,
Dreaming of past friendly garden walks,
And youthful tennis games and talks.

They reminisce the joy of soccer games,
Basketball, cricket and netball dates.
Enchanted by musical practising bands
And imitating singers of all genres.

Absent from the old Roseau bridge,
Is the scene we once gleefully rigged.
Sheets, pillow cases, pants and shirts
Bleaching out on boulders and dirt.

Yelling boys in their child birth garbs,
Teasing and taking clumsy head dives
Through deep river streams gushing by
Trying to outperform the burbling banks.

The traffic is now crazy. A furious din,
Honking and shouting from SUVs,
A nation gone wild. Too many cars
Replacing half-a-dozen longed for hire.

In past days, horse, buggy and man
Cleared roadways off delinquents and trash.
Instructions to horse were unambiguous
"Ho!" to move and "Ha!" to stop.

While her majesty's prisoners cleared
Public grounds from weeds and brush,
To the curiosity of school children
Who stood, stared then scampered off.

Name calling was their main mode of fun.
Hesketh greeted friends with "Hello Man!"
Twist called her gypsy dancer from *Zurika.*
Zabim hauled bails of cloth for Sylvia.

Debouyé urged to move to help himself,
Bishop Morris poked us as *zanfans Mederick.*
Sir Louis visibly enjoyed his daily walks.
All knew something about someone else.

Richard once sold *pistach* from his bicycle,
Bouboy and Farrell sold accras from trays.
Josephine graced weddings and served cocktails.
And Taste Me plied her ice cream and cakes.

Diana played the nights with dances and grog.
As Clemanté preached the bible by *boukan* torch.
Zaboka prepared for his major career move
Of leading compatriots by his political views.

Gossip was rampant with no telling of truth.
They wove a likely story too hard to refute.
Freedom of speech they claimed as their right.
With proclamation, "No name, no warrant."

Some were made to feel small and ashamed.
That was how they played their favorite game.
Disapproval on all sides. Pleasing no one.
Could care less about whom they wronged.

Begetting a child out of wedlock law,
Then the biggest human shameful draw.
Especially by some who themselves bi-blows
Were begotten outside the marriage docks.

Values have changed. Thinking is different.
The ancient class structure is now melding
Into a growing middle class of academia.
Most are encouraged to higher folklore.

Creole culture now came to the fore
With the advent of icon Mabel Caudeiron.
Exchanging current ignorance in favour of
Creole food, fashion, music and patois.

Do we wish the old city had remained the same?
Free from congestion, dodging busy strife?
When its main aim is to be progressively rife,
Move with the times and developing sites?

Developed nations give bike lanes and parks,
Designated parking spaces and metered spots.
Traffic signs saying stop, go and no thruways.
And sidewalks open to pedestrians and prams.

Developed nations hold daily entertainment,
Classical symphonies in subways and stops,
Delightful minstrels serenading passers-by,
And outdoor eateries midst flowers and plants,

Intolerable are noises disturbing the peace,
Unlicensed music blasting throughout towns,
Unprovoked aggression, quarrels and fights
And abuse of seniors, disabled and the young.

The new city will gain its due accolades
When respect becomes a normal way of life,
And persons move unencumbered and light.
What a joy this new attitudes could delight !

***

Naming

After several years of silence,
We reconnected on Facebook.
She charmed with golden looks
Reminiscent of easy mannerisms.
It seems nothing ever fazed her.
She always looked in control,
Managing quietly and competently,
So cool, collected and pleasantly.

I looked out at the blooming field,
Extending as far as the eyes could see.
Sparkling in the sunshine with brown eyes
So serene, so beautiful, so golden
Were the blooms called Brown-eyed Susan.
Was my friend, Susan, so named
As her personality and demeanor
Mimicked the field of lazy Susan?
Or did she adopt the characteristics
Of her namesake with bright eyes?

I tested my name to see if indeed
My name and personality were in sync,
Lor and rain. Before I got any highfalutin
Ideas that my name implies my
Receiving grand showers of gold and pearls,
I was quickly grounded by the controls
Set by the main germs of Germaine
And the gentle iron fist of Jennifer
To stay in line and in check.

Labelle thinks she has the most
Beautiful life as her name implies.
Anne embodies man and is the
Kindest of all humans. Both content
As to how they conduct their lives.
What do you say your name means?
Do you feel an affiliation with those
With whom you share the same name?

Just feel the exhilaration of Gillian-Chantelle
As she skips and dances to all songs.
Are names recorded in prenatal books;
Lives ensconced in eternal nooks;
Souls enjoined for an afterlife look;
Spirits commingle in the daily souk?
Our names are given for our best lives now.
Just a glimpse of whom and what we are
And whom and what we can become.

Brown-eyed Susan

Strange Pronouncement

They were all curiously amused,
Looking on with smiles bemused.
Some sympathetic, some amazed,
Some with broad grins unfazed.
Awaited the ultimate proclaim.

"I am your husband," he proclaimed.
A giant man came in the subway car
And sat down right next to her.
He wore a hard hat and work boots
And carried an extra-large lunch spoof.

Surprised, she interrupted her reading,
Lifted her head from her mobile probing.
"I am your husband," he announced.
"Where are you coming from?"
Sternness in his firm voice.

His direct gaze drew out her reply.
"Work!" she answered quite shortly,
Not wishing to engage much further.
"Where are you going?" he asked coyly.
"Home!" she spoke evasively,

Hoping to avoid more questionings.
"Yes, go home, I am coming soon,"
He continued in no-nonsense tones.
"I am her husband." He informed the riders.
"I am her husband and want her to go home."

Wanting to attract her full attention,
He turned to her again and said,
"Go home, I am coming to join you soon,
"Then we will go to the park for a nice walk."

He continued this ranting until the next stop.
Thankfully, her stop was the next station.
"Bye, bye, I am coming soon," he chanted
"I am her husband!" he continuously blurted.

She prayed that he would not alight
And follow her home in growing twilight.
"Bye," she answered with a brave smile
And a wave saying. "Have a good night,"
As his voice with his bold announcement
Followed her until the train moved off.

She wondered how long did he continue
This declaration? Did he have a new
Proclamation? Who was the recipient
Of his next proposal or was he just having
Fun at the expense of humourless riders?

***

Calling For Help

She came out of the building yelling.
Calling on a deity to take her bidding
Desperation and anguish in her telling.
She screamed out her mother, "Mama!"
She called out for her father, "Papa!"
"Where are you? I want you. Now!"

She jumped up and down the city street.
Ran several times then stamped her feet.
Hauled her knapsack off her back.
Threw it on the ground, resumed her attack.
Huge giant sobs as if her heart would break.

She leapt towards an open door.
Determinedly knocked many times,
Continuing her heartbreaking cries.
No answer made her furiously wild.
An uncontrollable rage shook her.

She lifted her head to the skies,
Letting out a gross animal wail.
Grabbed up her bag from the ground,
Threw it furiously against the door.
She was totally out of control.

Passers-by gave her a wide berth.
Scared to watch or to approach.
Rage filled her. Tears ran down her face.
Rage and tears enveloped her being
Everyone looked in awe and disbelief.

What did this young girl ingest
To create in herself such digest?
Had she been in that place before,
One of the several new pop-up stores
Selling pharma and lollipops?

From such doors she had emerged.
Is her curiousity now satisfied?
Does she desire more disastrous tolls?
Anyone close-by for a helping hand?
Who ever dares approach her kind?

She continued her anguished walk
And finally entered a grocery store,
To do what I will never know,
Leaving shoppers shaking their heads
Disbelieving a scene never before held.

There are varying degrees of disharmony,
Behaviours congruent with dichotomy.
Extraordinary in their various deliveries,
Inexplicable in their peculiar renderings.
And flamboyant in manners and dress.

Do they just wish to be seen and heard?
Do they just need to fill an empty void?
Is this their call for love and acceptance?
Are we, humans paying much attention?
How similar are our needs for protection?

Answers already contained in oneself.
To be questioned, probed and extracted.
When desire and opportunity shine light
On the need to end senseless growing strife,
To learn and explore how bright is life.

***

The Art of Living

A wide world of countless possibilities
Requiring life to satisfy these capabilities.
Life is as diverse as its many abilities.
Living seems fraught with responsibilities.

Responsibilities are to be taken seriously,
Otherwise, they could become heavy liabilities
Of how unconsciously we conduct our living
And account for that which is missing.

Each day commences with activities.
Committed events must be completed.
Targeted goals move towards fulfillment.
Ordinary happenings performed with strain.

Why is there strain performing these events?
Unrealistic expectations in commitments;
Unwillingness to move with targeted goals;
Inadequate planning to accomplish all?

Those events are very well intentioned.
And bring with them many contentions.
But can we deliver all as mentioned
Without the ego causing much detention?

The ego thrives on intense competition.
Pitting wills to cause major confusion.
Invariably making strong judgements
Right or wrong its main pronouncements.

Inflexible behaviour is its cause and cue.
Chaotic thinking its reason and due.
Renders inefficient its many executions.
And insufficient its entire acquisitions.

How can we be efficient and sufficient,
And willingly be aware and content,
And consciously focus on the moment
Dealing with the insistence of the ego?

Many issues to deal with constantly
Needing the artist's creative strategy
To shift, rearrange according to priority,
Disallowing the ego to wreck its beauty.

The artist diligently prepares materials,
Aligning in priority of use and *arils*.
Painters apply paints for best effects.
Singers practise a piece until perfect.

Artists craft their work for best outcome
Shifting and moulding to what it can become.
The art of crafting is a gift we all share
Through our humanness imbued in nature.

Moulding the art is uneasy and incomplete.
Art is not perfect but true to its form.
The truth of the art is in its individuality
Expressed in unique forms of ingenuity.

Acts of ingenuity affirm fervent humanity.
Willing awareness guides errant humility.
Both linked by the inspired connecting hum
To create the magic art of living datum.

The hum generously loaded with living acts,
Donning artistic expressions in varying darts,
Taking its liberal cue from bounteous nature,
As it copiously distributes to living creatures.

Nature gifted trees and branches to sway
In the breeze and bend with strong winds.
It caused a hierarchy of the animal kingdom
To ensure survival of the fittest of the species.

So too, it requires that humans be flexible
In their dealings with all that is and rearrange
Thoughts and deeds in congruence with nature
To experience the true art of human living.

To be alive and aware is to be truly human.
Physically breathing in the good there is.
Deliberately breathing out negative energies,
Renewing and rejuvenating all our cells.

Renewal and rejuvenation come with promises.
Acceptance of situations as they happen;
Enthusiasm to deal consciously with what is;
Enjoyment of pleasure in the present moment.

Fulfillment of these promises can occur
When we live them in the present moment.
Schooling the ego not to dwell in the past
And not to project into the distant future.

To be fully engaged is the art of living
Extending humility towards all humanity;
Forgiving judgements with flexibility;
Dealing courageously with insensitivity.

When we acknowledge our human failings,
We treat ourselves with gentle kindness
Which responds with compassionate figures
That better understand our human nature.

When we feel empathy in relationships,
And see others no different from ourselves,
We better express and uphold the human spirit
That furthers within ourselves the art of living.

Art of living suggests connecting with humans,
Holding ourselves as mirrors for each other.
When cracked, signal a broken call to love.
When whole, reflect the light of possibilities.

**

The Fall

Slippery roads need more caution.
Broken pavements warn attention.
Paying heed carefully progressed
In four decades never transgressed.

Dry weather promotes confidence.
Clear walkways support advancement.
Moving carelessly and heedlessly,
She lets down her perpetual defence.

Kicked her foot against the mound,
Found herself prone on the ground.
Surprised that she is unable to rise
Wondering that's not me so demised!

Surprised to find herself so humbled,
Requiring assistance to break the tumble.
Handbag of nick knacks strewn apace.
Eye glasses sitting firmly on her face.

The shock seems greater than the fall.
Body immobile on the paving stone.
Wondering how did this happen at all
She mentally tested for broken bones.

Her high falls occur at ordinary times
When things seem normal and aligned,
Multiple thoughts occupying her mind
Throw care and caution to the wind.

Moving fast to hold shutting doors,
Like rushing was her only choice.
Slipped as doors closed in her prance,
Halting what was a graceful entrance.

Impatience awaiting doors to open again,
Regardless of opportunities to regain,
Unwilling to maintain a reasonable pace,
Could surely have us fall flat on our face

***

Celebration

Loved ones celebrate deaths of the departed.
Milestones commemorated since we started.
Birth days, etcetera feted in refinement.
We honour most others' special events.
When do we celebrate our own aliveness?

Sometimes we think our lives are so dread,
Nothing accomplished, nothing read.
Unfulfilled desires to have something else.
Dissatisfaction with where we are and when.
Wanting somewhere exciting, someone new.

Moping around for grand happenstance,
Awaiting probability of their occurrence,
We miss the beauty of little things around.
Little things which pervade daily living
Worthy of acknowledgement and celebrating.

Buried in little things are daily cares,
Infused by senseless futile intrusions,
Energy sapping, persistent mind-nagging.
To the exclusion of rightful thinking,
An appreciation of beauty, light and joy.

Little things, a source of constant jubilation
Are so many for a cause of daily celebration.
When spirit is riffed with positive intentions,
And the mind focused on earnest execution,
These give openings for expressive celebrations.

Positive intentions are strengthened by affirmations.
Earnest execution achieved by focused repetitions.
New learning requires constant memorization.
Efficient application demands mindful retention.
Celebration requests affirmation and repetition.

Intention is prayerful request for the desired.
A wish to prepare delicious meals for loved ones,
With all the ingredients and a focus of love,
Celebration of preparedness and sharing begin.
Everything done with love sings of celebrating.

When situations intrude on our ability to focus
And hamper our good intentions and execution,
We need to change our mindset to one of joy.
With recognition, acknowledgement and acceptance
That which exists is ultimately beyond control.

However, persistent negative intrusions inform,
Preventing the experience of joy to conform
Into expressions of innate celebratory living.
We then pull out our bag of affirmation bricks
In search for already-developed mantra tricks.

Let ever-ready mantra change your mood.
Let repetition permeate until all is good.
Replace feelings and thoughts with "I am…"
Beauty, love, happy, joy, faith, abundant,
I am secure and above all "I am grateful!"

The great "I am" is gratitude for aliveness.
An aliveness that only you can experience.
An aliveness that concedes and recedes.
And transforms improbable into probable,
As you evoke the mantra of repetitive, "I am…."

Gratitude is response to gracious giving.
Aliveness is the gift for open receiving.
To be alive in gratitude increases awareness.
Alive in gratitude multiplies joyousness,
A minutely daily celebration of live.

***

Spring

Hunkered down in underground beds,
They laid low and fallow.
Plotting and planning their every move
For a mighty resurgence and hello!
Marvellous surprise upspring to follow.
They whispered about the splendour
Of their gorgeous variegated blooms.
They boasted of prankish sprinkling
Jasmine perfumes throughout rooms.
They scoffed away large expanse
Of wild fields awaiting attention.
They could already sense the velvet touch
Of wind rustling through their trees.
And feel the gentle tears of rain
Soothing their delicate boughs and leaves.
They anticipated the warmth of daytime sun
Scorching through their winter roots.
They perceived that that was only
The beginning of a renewed truce.
As they awaited the call of nature,
Its creatures and tools that said
It was safe to come out of hiding and live.

The last snow fall, a turbulent downpour,
Slyly signaled the time was right.
Without much ado, they gathered forces
To spring a surprise attack.
Bulbs spontaneously shot curious tips,
Defiantly challenging other plants to quip.
Giant trees wishing not to be outdone
Sprouted baby leaves for all along.
Simultaneous displays in coming days.
Crocuses hailed dandelions, saluted tulips.

Daffodils sang among wild flowers.
All in a cornucopia of brilliance,
Taking our breath away at the striking
Beauty and splendour and sounds.
Then releasing that breath in disbelief,
Leaving us awestruck in amazement.
Springing in enthralled appreciation
At how suddenly everything bloomed.
Undeniably humbled by our place
In this great scheme of the universe.
A proliferation of the gracious Creator
Calling upon all its living creatures
To spring forth in joyous rebirth.

Springing

Abundance

All that we need,
Already provided for us.
Just look around, see.
Savour the abundance.
It is all so free.
Tally the things around
Where abundance abound.
Accept and receive.
Give thanks for these
And lots more to come.

Gratitude opens the heart
For fair exchange.
Give according to your beget.
Nature supplies the rest.
Generosity and abundance,
Its greatest behest.
And graciously multiplies
What you give and get.
Be mindful of your protests.

Protests limit the general flow.
No room to give and to grow.
Let heartfelt service be your plight.
The multiplier take up your fight.
Work well your product and your pace.
Rise above shallow disgrace.
Discard thoughts that embrace
Poverty and limitations of race.

Abundance is our rightful due.
Love, health, wealth, success,
Happiness, freedom and joy.
Its very source is within ourselves
In collaboration with the deity within
Gifts and blessings awaiting.

Singing My Song

Lorraine Dorival

Coaching Discussions

Coaching has long been used in sporting professions and artistic performances. Over the past two decades, there has been a growing interest by corporations, business professionals and individuals desiring to make positive changes in their establishments and lives. Coaching is a specific skill which assists participants move from point A to point B in human endeavours. It is a collaboration between coach and client. The poetry collection "More than Okay" is the continuing conversation addressing my journey as well as what I have gleaned through working with some clients. The collection contains various expressions intended for wellness, healing and growth. The following exercise is an invitation to coach yourself and others using the poetry and questions in an attempt to make life more enjoyable, productive and fulfilling.

Small Trials are a collection of experiences and observations which cloud our reasoning.
Questions: What small trials are clouding your reasoning?
What are you doing to obliterate these trials?

Writing My Poems looks at the inspiration behind and method of my writing.
Questions: What are your personal expressions of creativity?
Discuss how you execute them and how they make you feel.

Undeserved Punishment touches upon misconceptions of a situation and the ensuing reactions which could led to both physical and psychological abuses.
Questions: How have you been misjudged?
What was the outcome?

Crossing Over deals with the tenacity with which we approach obstacles when we want to make positive changes in life.
Questions: How willing are you to make changes in your life?
How will you deal with the obstacles in your way?

The Park gives me such pleasure. It is my favorite place to walk for exercise, people watch and rejuvenate. It is so beneficial to have a park as part of your neighbourhood.

Questions: What do you do in your park near-by?

What are the sights and sounds which edify your senses in the park?

Carnival is a cultural annual festivity during which participants express their creativity in music, song, dance, food, fashion, costumes and everything else.

Questions: What are your chief expressions of community activity?

How do you participate? What does participation feel like?

Sister Mary Theophana was a catholic nun who taught in our high school.

She had such a *joie de vivre* that she inspired us to be the best we could. She mentored us and challenged us to think outside the box.

Questions: How significant was your mentor during your youth?

How has the influence of that mentorship served you throughout your life?

Perception is a feeling or thought that things are not just as they seem. Generally, we take the good that comes our way as granted, not caring too much about their origin.

Questions: What gifts have you received lately?

What are your thoughts about the gifts? Explain.

Second Chance discusses the changes necessary for a successful second chance or a new way of life away from the former life.

Questions: What situations you encountered which require a second chance?

What are the considerations for the success of your second chance?

True Confessions is a humorous look at youthful flirtations which could make lifelong impressions.

Questions: What impressions of your youthful flirtations remain?
How do view these impressions today/now?

The Fall shows that when you move full force with impatience, disregarding warnings and pushing aside what could be in the way, you could be in for a fall.

Questions: What has been the outcome whenever you dropped your guard?
What did you learn from the outcome?

Caution is the time you take to pay attention to your way of being and your environment and a commitment to improve both.

Questions: What improvements you see are required in your environment?
What is your commitment to help make these improvements?

Passing Away: It has been so sad lately. Lots of our friends have died and gone to their eternal rest.

Questions: What was your relationship with someone who has died?
What would you like to say to that someone?

It's Okay encourages you to be kind to yourself. Every situation in life, although challenging, is intended for your healing and growth.

Questions: What are the challenges you currently face?
How are you learning to resolve them?

Comfort is a necessity in our lives. We look for it from others and we give it to others and sometimes we withhold it from others and ourselves.

Questions: When are you most in need of comfort?
How do you express that need? Is that expression working for you?

The Absent Father shows that although the father had good intentions, he may have been absent both physically and emotionally.

Questions: How did your father behave in his house?

What do you wish you had received from your father?

Time Revealed observes the nuances with which some persons struggle. Some behaviours are unconscious and should be brought to the fore. Others require awareness to see their effect on others.

Questions: How aware are you that your behaviour has an effect?

How would you qualify the effect you have on others?

Aloneness is very profound in its solitude and appreciates the opportunities to be at one with nature and be allowed to think and create.

Questions: What do you think of your aloneness?

What do you sense and think when alone?

Roasted Ground Beans describes the daily devotion of two grandmothers. The love and care they gave to their grandchildren and their occupation of grinding roasted coffee and cocoa beans.

Questions: What are your fond memories of older family members?

What notable new memories are you making with your family members?

Old Age is a humorous conversation between two elderly past lovers. They reminisce about their love, friends and activities.

Questions: What humorous events can you recall?

What feelings do these events evoke?

My Mother was the most influential person in my life. I learned from her both negative and positive. In later years when I realized that our lives differ, if I wanted to be authentic, I had to develop my own personality.

Questions: What stands out in your relationship with your guardian?

What were the positive and negative impact of that guardianship?

Mistakes happen when we are not attentive in the present moment. Mistakes also happen when an outcome is unexpected.
Questions: When are you likely to make mistakes?
How can you avoid such mistakes in the future?

The Romantic Soul yearns for couples to bring back spark and liveliness and love back in their relationships.
Questions: What can you do to show love and caring in your relationship?
How would you feel in such a relationship?

Memory is the working of the brain to bring the past into the present moment.
The events of the past are necessary for our learning and growth, not to relive pain and suffering.
Questions: How often during the day does your memory go in the past?
How willing are you to forgive the events that you relive?

Creole is a culture established by European and Africans in the Americas after the abolishment of slavery. It brings its people together in celebration at specific times showcasing its creativity in food, dress, music, song, dance and language.
Questions: How do you celebrate your culture?
What part do you play in its celebration?

Birds come to visit me frequently. I envy their freedom, how they just spread their wings and fly in unity and seemingly learned discipline.
Questions: What do you learn from your favourite animal friend?
How do you implement that learning?

Credo is the belief that life holds countless possibilities and each person needs to recognize their own possibilities in the grand scheme of things.

Questions: What are your possibilities?

What are you doing to manifest these possibilities?

The New City 2020 is very different from the old. So much has changed and draws much nostalgia and a longing for the old city and more discipline.

Questions: What are the changes you see in your city?

Write an appreciation of your city.

Myths and Legends are a collection of incredible folk tales which convey profound underlying teachings.

Questions: What other myths and legends do you know?

What have you learned from these myths and legends?

Naming looks at the light side of how names suit the nominee and whether those names are preordained.

Questions: what do you think your name means?

How does your name synchronize with your personality?

Strange Pronouncement is a story of a man making unusual claims of a relationship to the amusement and amazement of the riding audience.

Questions: What is amusing about this pronouncement?

How would you interpret this pronouncement?

Calling for Help is the story of a young girl whose resulting experience from ingesting a substance was different from her expectations.

Questions: Give an example where your experience differed from your expectations.

How did you resolve your expectations?

The Art of Living is the practice of treating yourself as a human being as well as treating others likewise. This practice is humility.
Questions: What is it like treating yourself as a human being?
How do you practise humility?

Celebration highlights the simple things in life which bring pleasure and should be daily celebrated with gratitude and joy.
Questions: What are the little things worthy of your daily celebration?
How do you daily celebrate those little things?

The Hurricane hits some Islands and continents almost every year and leaves lots of destruction and misery in its wake.
Questions: What is your experience of a hurricane?
How has this experience influence your thinking?

Spring is a time of resurgence and rebirth. We all experience various seasons in our lives during which we languish in idleness, immobility and being generally unmotivated.
Questions: What are the blocks and fears obstructing your rebirth ?
What are your plans to remove these blocks and fears?

Abundance is all around us in what we already own and our ability to earn. We must forever be grateful for both. So, the light will shine on our ways to what is a need and the extent of our wants.
Questions: What is your most urgent need today?
What are your doing to acquire it?

Glossary

Arils	Husks, skins
Bèlè	Tradition French dance
Bèlè Soté	Tradition French dance
Boukan	Open fire
Bonm kalalou	Pot of soup with crabs and smoked meats
Boumboum	Tradition musical instrument
Chakchak	Traditional percussion
Débouyé	To help oneself
Droop	Hang out
Dwiyèt	Traditional creole dress for women
Fête	Festivity or party
Glorisida	Glory Cedar tree
Gwaj	Musical instrument
Joie de vivre	Joyful living
Jing ping	Musical band
Jip	Traditional creole skirt
Jipon	Petticoat
Koubouyon pwéson	Fish cooked in a sauce or broth
Kanèl	Cinnamon
Kwéyòl	Creole
Laligne	Folklore mermaid
Ladjé	Spread out
La Femme Creole	Creole woman
Lapo Kabwit	Goat skin
Lavwé	Chorus, choral group
Les Creole	Creole folk
Loogaroo	Folklore werewolf
Mazouk	Traditional European dance
Mederick	Our Grandfather
Mélé mélange	A mix up
Patwa	Patois, broken French

Pistach	Peanuts
Ponme kanèl	Stylish earrings in shape of an apple
Pwéson	Fish
Quadrille	Traditional European dance
San sigwèté	Exposed
Souk	Marketplace
Soucouyant	Folklore witch
Tètkassé	Woman's headpiece in traditional dress
Wòb dwiyèt	Traditional Creole dress for women
Wòb	Derivative of traditional dress
Zabim	Bright-eyed
Zanfans	Children
Zurika	A theatrical play

Printed in the United States
by Baker & Taylor Publisher Services